A
TO SOULS

Words of Our Lord from
THE WAY OF DIVINE LOVE
of Sister Josefa Menéndez

> *"Never shall I weary of repentant sinners, nor cease from hoping for their return, and the greater their distress, the greater My welcome."*
> —Words of Our Lord
> (See p. 2)

TAN BOOKS AND PUBLISHERS, INC.
Rockford, Illinois 61105

Nihil obstat: Patrick Morris, S.T.D., L.S.S.
Censor deputatus

Imprimatur: E. Morrogh Bernard
Vicar General
Westminster
October 11, 1949

Originally published by Sands & Co., Ltd., London & Glasgow, in approximately 1949. Retypeset and republished by TAN Books and Publishers, Inc. in 1998.

ISBN 0-89555-614-6

Cover illustration: B. F., France. (c/c, 5630). 0 100LE, New York.

Printed and bound in the United States of America.

TAN BOOKS AND PUBLISHERS, INC.
P.O. Box 424
Rockford, Illinois 61105
1998

"I want souls to have confidence in My mercy, to expect all from My clemency, and never to doubt My readiness to forgive."

—Words of Our Lord

INTRODUCTION

This booklet contains passages drawn from the Message entrusted by Our Lord to Sister Josefa Menéndez, coadjutrix sister of the Society of the Sacred Heart.[1]

Hidden in the silence of her convent "Les Feuillants" (Poitiers, France), this humble sister who had left her home in Spain to follow her vocation became the chosen instrument of Love.

Jesus, His Heart on fire, revealed Himself to her, spoke to her, molded her as He pleased and gave her a share in His work of redemption. Then He entrusted His desires to her and asked her to transmit them to the world.

The aim of this little book is to respond to that appeal by spreading the Message to the many faithful souls who have been chosen by Our Lord and are consecrated to Him.

So, may they all accept and read the message; may they find in it light and strength for each day as it comes; may they become collaborators in this work of love; may they be fuel for the fire that Our Lord came to enkindle throughout the

---

1. Sister Josefa Menéndez, *The Way of Divine Love, or The Message of the Sacred Heart to the World* (London and Glasgow: Sands & Co., Ltd., 1949; TAN, 1972 and 1981).

whole earth; and according to His desire may they form a chain of souls whose hearts will be more and more on fire with love, love that trusts and expects everything from Him, so that, aflame with this fire, they will communicate it to the whole world.

A CALL TO SOULS

"I am *Love!* My Heart can no longer contain its devouring flames. I love souls so dearly that I have sacrificed My life for them.

"It is this love that keeps Me a prisoner in the tabernacle. For nearly twenty centuries I have dwelt there, night and day, veiled under the species of Bread and concealed in the small white Host, bearing through love, neglect, solitude, contempt, blasphemies, outrages, sacrileges . . .

"For love of souls, I instituted the Sacrament of Penance, that I might forgive them, not once or twice, but as often as they need it to recover grace. There I wait for them, longing to wash away their sins, not in water, but in My Blood.

"How often in the course of the ages have I, in one way or another, made known My love for men: I have shown them how ardently I desire their salvation. I have revealed My Heart to them. This devotion has been as light cast over the whole earth, and today by its means those who labor to gain souls to My service have been enabled to do so.

"Now, I want something more, for if I long for love in response to My own, this is not the only return I desire from souls: I want them all to have confidence in My mercy, to expect all from My clemency, and never to doubt My readiness to forgive.

"I am God, but a God of love! I am a Father, but a Father full of compassion and never harsh. My Heart is infinitely holy but also infinitely wise, and knowing human frailty and infirmity, stoops to poor sinners with infinite mercy.

"I love those who after a first fall come to Me for pardon . . . I love them still more when they beg pardon for their second sin, and should this happen again, I do not say a million times but a million million times, I still love them and pardon them, and I will wash in My Blood their last as fully as their first sin.

"Never shall I weary of repentant sinners, nor cease from hoping for their return, and the greater their distress, the greater My welcome. Does not a father love a sick child with special affection? Are not his care and solicitude greater? So is the tenderness and compassion of My Heart more abundant for sinners than for the just.

"This is what I wish all to know. I will teach sinners that the mercy of My Heart is inexhaustible. Let the callous and indifferent know that My Heart is a fire which will enkindle them, because I love them. To devout and saintly souls I would be "The Way," that making great strides in perfection, they may safely reach the harbor of eternal beatitude. Lastly, of consecrated souls, priests and religious, My elect and chosen ones, I ask, once more, all their love and that they should not doubt Mine, but above all that they should trust Me and never doubt My mercy. It is so easy to trust completely in My Heart."

(June 11, 1923).

"I will make it known that My work rests on nothingness and misery—such is the first link in the chain of love that I have prepared for souls from eternity. I will use you to show that I love misery, littleness and absolute nothingness.

"I will reveal to souls the excess of My love and how far I will go in forgiveness, and how even their faults will be used by Me with blind indulgence . . . yes, write . . . with blind indulgence. I see depths, the very depths of souls, I see how they fain would please, console and glorify Me, and the act of humility they are obliged to make when they see themselves so feeble, is solace and glory to My Heart. What does their helplessness matter? Cannot I supply all their deficiencies? I will show how My Heart uses their very weakness to give life to many souls that have lost it.

"I will make known that the measure of My love and mercy for fallen souls is limitless. I want to forgive them. It rests Me to forgive. I am ever there, waiting, with boundless love till souls come to Me. Let them come, nor be discouraged. Let them fearlessly throw themselves into My arms! I am their Father.

"Many of My religious do not understand all they can do to draw those steeped in ignorance to My Heart. They do not know how I yearn to draw them to Myself and give them life . . . true life.

"Yes, Josefa, I will teach you the secrets of My love, and you will be a living example of My mercy, for if I have such love and predilection for you who are of no account whatever, what am I not ready to do for others more generous than you?"   (August 6, 1922).

"Come . . . enter My Heart. How easy it is for a mere nothing to lose itself in that abyss of love.

"That is how I will consume your littleness and nothingness.

"I will act through you, speak through you, and make Myself known through you. How many will find life in My words! How many will take new courage as they understand the fruit to be drawn from their efforts! A little act of generosity, of patience, of poverty . . . may become treasure that will win a great number of souls to My Heart . . ."

(August 7, 1922).

"I do not look at the act itself, I look at the intention. The smallest act, if done out of love, acquires such merit that it gives Me immense consolation . . . I want only love, I ask for nothing else."

(September 8, 1922).

"When a soul is generous enough to give Me all I ask, she gathers up treasure for herself and others and snatches great numbers of souls from perdition. It is by their sacrifices and their love that My chosen souls are deputed by My Heart to dispense My graces to mankind. The world is full of perils . . . How many poor souls are dragged towards sin and constantly need a visible or invisible help! Ah! let Me say it again, do My chosen souls know of what treasures they deprive themselves and others, when they are ungenerous? I do not say that by the fact of My choice, a soul is freed from her faults and wretchedness. That soul may and will fall often again, but if she humbles herself, if she recognizes her nothingness, if she tries to repair her faults by little acts of generosity and love, if she confides and surrenders herself once more to My Heart . . . she gives Me more glory and can do more good to other souls, than if she had never fallen. Miseries and weaknesses are of no consequence, what I do ask of them is love.

"Yes, in spite of its miseries, a soul can love Me to folly . . . But realize that I am speaking only of faults of frailty and inadvertence, not of willed sin or voluntary infidelity.

"Offer your life, imperfect as it is, that all My chosen souls may realize the beautiful mission that they can carry out through their ordinary actions and in their daily struggles. Let them never forget that I have preferred them to so many others, not because of their goodness, but because of their wretchedness . . . I am all love, and that flame in Me consumes all their weakness.

"I will again tell you the secrets of My Heart . . . But the desire which consumes Me is ever the same: It is that souls may know My Heart better and better."   (October 20, 1922).

"Write for My souls:

"The soul who constantly unites her life with Mine glorifies Me and does a great work for souls. Thus, if engaged in work of no value in itself . . . if she bathes it in My Blood or unites it to the work I Myself did during My mortal life, it will greatly profit souls . . . more perhaps, than if she had preached to the whole world . . . and that, whether she studies, speaks or writes . . . whether she sews, sweeps or rests . . . provided first that the act is sanctioned by obedience or duty and not done from mere caprice; secondly: that it is done in intimate union with Me, with great purity of intention and covered with My Blood.

"I so much want souls to understand this! It is not the action in itself that is of value; it is the intention with which it is done. When I swept and labored in the workshop of Nazareth, I gave as much glory to My Father as when I preached during My Public Life.

"There are many souls who in the eyes of the world fill important posts and they give My Heart great glory; this is true. But I have many hidden souls who in their humble labors are very useful workers in My vineyard, for they are moved by love, and they know how to cover their deeds with supernatural gold by bathing them in My Blood. My love goes so far that My souls can draw great treasure out of mere nothing. When as soon as they wake they unite themselves to Me and offer their whole day with a burning desire that My Heart may use it for the profit of souls . . . when with love they perform their duties, hour by hour and moment by moment . . . How great is the treasure they amass in one day!

"I will reveal My love to them more and more . . . it is inexhaustible and how easy it is for a loving soul to let itself be guided by Love."

(November 30, 1922).

"Write for souls:

"My Heart is all love and it embraces all souls, but how can I make My chosen souls understand My special love for them and how I wish to use them to save sinners and so many souls who are exposed to the perils of the world? For this reason I would like them to know how much I desire their perfection, and that it consists in doing their ordinary actions in intimate union with Me. If they once grasped this, they could divinize their life and all their activities by this close union with My Heart . . . and how great is the value of a divinized day!

"When a soul is burnt up with desire to love, nothing is a burden to her, but if she feels cold and spiritless everything becomes hard and difficult . . . let her then come to My Heart to revive her courage . . . Let her offer Me her dejection, and unite it to My fervor; then she may rest content, for her day will be of incomparable value to souls. All human miseries are known to My Heart, and My compassion for them is great.

"But I desire souls to unite themselves to Me not only in a general way. I long for this union to be constant and intimate, as it is between friends who live together: for even if they are not talking all the time, at least they look at each other, and their mutual affectionate little kindnesses are the fruit of their love.

"When a soul is in peace and consolation, doubtless it is easier for her to think of Me, but if she is in the throes of desolation and anguish, she need not fear. I am content with a glance. I understand, and this mere look will draw down on her special proofs of My tenderness.

"I will repeat again to souls how My Heart loves them . . . for I want them to know Me thoroughly, that they may make Me known to those I place in their care.

"I ardently desire My chosen souls to fix their eyes on Me, and never turn them away . . . and among them there should be no mediocrity which usually is the result of a misunderstanding of My love. No! it is neither difficult nor hard to love My Heart, but on the contrary, it is sweet and easy. They need do nothing extraordinary to attain to a high degree of love: purity of intention, be the action great or small . . . intimate union with My Heart, and love will do the rest."

(December 2, 1922).

"Yes, I am that Jesus who loves souls tenderly . . . Behold this Heart that never ceases calling them, guarding them, and caring for them . . . Behold this Heart on fire with longing for their love, but especially for the love of My chosen ones.

"Write, write more for them:

"My Heart is not only an abyss of love, It is also an abyss of mercy; and knowing as I do that even My closest friends are not exempt from human frailties, I will take each of their actions, however insignificant, to be clothed through Me with immense value for the help of those in need and for the salvation of sinners.

"All cannot preach nor evangelize distant uncivilized peoples, but all, yes, all, can make My Heart known and loved . . . All can mutually help one another to increase the number of the saved by preventing the loss of many souls . . . and that, through My love and mercy.

"I will tell My chosen souls that My love for them goes further still; not only shall I make use of their daily life and of their least actions, but I will make use of their very wretchedness . . . their frailties . . . even of their falls for the salvation of souls.

"Love transforms and divinizes everything and mercy pardons all."   (December 5, 1922).

". . . Write a few more words for My souls:

"Love transforms their most ordinary actions and gives them an infinite value, but it does more: My Heart loves My chosen souls so tenderly, that I wish to use their miseries, their weaknesses, and often even their faults.

"Souls that see themselves overwhelmed with miseries, attribute nothing good to themselves, and their very abjectness clothes them with a certain humility that they would not have if they saw themselves to be less imperfect.

"When therefore in the course of apostolic work or in the carrying out of duties, a consciousness of their incapacity is forced upon them . . . or when they experience a kind of repugnance to helping souls towards perfection to which they know themselves to be still strangers, such souls are compelled to humble themselves in the dust, and should this self-knowledge impel them to My feet, asking pardon for their halting efforts, begging of My Heart the strength and courage they need, it is hardly possible for them to conceive how lovingly My Heart goes out to them and how marvellously fruitful I will make their labors.

"Those whose generosity is not equal to these daily endeavors and sacrifices will see their lives go by full only of promise which never comes to fruition.

"But in this, distinguish: to souls who habitually promise and yet do no violence to themselves nor prove their abnegation and love in any way I say: 'Beware lest all this straw and stubble which you have gathered into your barns take fire or be scattered in an instant by the wind!' But there are others, and it is of them I now speak, who begin their day with a very good will and desire to prove their love. They pledge themselves to self-denial or generosity in this or that circumstance . . . But when the time comes they are prevented by self-love, temperament, health, or I know not what, from carrying out what a few hours before they quite sincerely purposed to do. Nevertheless they speedily acknowledge their weakness and, filled with shame, beg for pardon, humble themselves, and renew their promise . . . Ah! Let them know that these souls please Me as much as if they had nothing with which to reproach themselves."[2] (December 12, 1922).

---

2. Our Lord here establishes a very clear distinction between habitual venial faults, unresisted and consented to, and faults of frailty that are repaired.

He explains that the willed reparation gives Him more comfort than the fault of frailty gave Him displeasure. In fact, the humility, confidence and generosity implied in an act of reparation presuppose awareness and complete consent of the will—a condition only partially fulfilled in the fault of frailty.

"I want to forgive. I want to reign over souls and pardon all nations. I want to rule souls, nations, the whole world. My peace must be extended over the entire universe, but in a special way over this dear country [France] where devotion to My Heart first took root . . . O that I might be its peace, its life, its King. I am Wisdom and Beatitude! I am Love and Mercy! I am Peace, I shall reign! I will shower My mercies on the world to wipe out its ingratitude. To make reparation for its crimes, I will choose victims who will obtain pardon . . . for there are in the world many whose desire is to please Me . . . and there are moreover generous souls who will sacrifice everything they possess, that I may use them according to My will and good pleasure.

"My reign will be one of peace and love and I shall inaugurate it by compassion on all: such is the end I have in view, and this is the great work of My love.

"My appeal is addressed to all: to those consecrated in religion and those living in the world, to the good and to sinners, to the learned and the illiterate, to those in authority and to those who obey. To each of them I come to say: if you seek happiness you will find it in Me. If riches, I am infinite wealth. If you desire peace, in Me alone is peace found. I am Mercy and Love! and I must be sovereign King.

". . . All My longing is to set souls on fire . . . those of the entire world . . . Alas! they turn from the flame, but I shall triumph, they will be Mine, and I shall be their King. Suffer with me, that the world may know Me and that souls may come to Me. It is by suffering that love will triumph."

(June 12, 1923).

"I want souls to let the true light penetrate them.

"I want children . . . those innocent hearts that do not know Me and grow up cold and indifferent, and ignorant of the value of their souls . . .! Yes, I want these young souls who are My delight to find a home where they are taught to know Me, taught to grow up in the fear of My law and the love of My Heart.

"I want to conquer hearts by the very strength of My love. I want to restore good morals, to raise and ennoble them so that men will live not merely for earth but for Heaven. This does not mean that I am against human progress. On the contrary, I long for men to increase their knowledge, their talents, their power, but I want them to realize how to unite divine with human knowledge, and in their search for earthly goods to recognize what makes souls really great and happy.

"I have chosen you to help Me in this work of love.

"I desire you to be fuel for the fire that I want

to enkindle throughout the whole earth, for it is useless to light a flame unless there is fuel to feed it . . .

"This is why I want to make a chain of souls whose hearts will be more and more on fire with love, love that trusts and expects everything from My Heart . . . so that they will communicate it to the whole world." (September 21-28, 1923).

"Do not imagine that I am going to speak to you of anything but My Cross. By it I saved the world; by it I will bring the world back to the truths of Faith and to the Way of Love . . .

"I will manifest My will to you: I saved the world from the Cross, that is to say through suffering. You know that sin is an infinite offense and needs infinite reparation . . . that is why I ask you to offer up your sufferings and labors, in union with the infinite merits of My Heart. You know that My Heart is yours. Take It, therefore, and repair by It . . . Instill love and trust into the souls that come in contact with you. Bathe them in love—bathe them in confidence in the goodness and mercy of My Heart. Whenever you can speak of Me and make Me known, tell them always not to fear, for I am a God of Love.

"I recommend three practices very specially to you:

First: The practice of the Holy Hour, because it is one of the ways by which an infinite reparation can be offered up to God the Father, through the mediation of Jesus Christ His Divine Son.

Second: The devotion of the five *Paters* [Our Fathers] in honor of My wounds, since through them the world was saved.

Third: Constant union, or rather daily offering of the merits of My Heart, because by doing so you will give to all your actions an infinite value.

"Unceasingly use My Life, My Blood, My Heart . . . confide constantly and without any fear in this Heart: this secret is known to few; I want you to know it and profit by it."

(October 15, 1923).

"I desire that My love should be the sun to enlighten and heat to reanimate souls. That is why My words must reach them. I want all the world to recognize in Me a God of mercy and of love. I wish that everywhere My desire to forgive and save souls should be read, and that not even the most wretched be kept back by fear! . . . nor the most guilty fly from Me . . . Let them all come. I await them with open arms like the most affectionate of fathers in order to impart life and true happiness to them.

"That the world may know My clemency, I need apostles who will reveal My Heart . . . but first these must know It themselves . . . otherwise how can they teach others?

"So for the next few days, I will speak for My priests, My religious and My nuns, that all may clearly understand what I require: I want them to form a league of love in order to teach and publish the love and mercy of My Heart to all men, even to the extremities of the world. I want the need and desire for reparation to be re-awakened and grow among faithful and chosen souls, for the world is full of sin . . . and at this present moment nations are arousing the wrath of God. But He desires His reign to be one of love, hence this appeal to chosen souls, especially those of this nationality. He asks them to repair, to obtain pardon, and above all to draw down grace on this country which, I repeat, was the first to know My Heart and spread devotion to It.

"I want the world to be saved . . . peace and union to prevail everywhere. It is My will to reign, and reign I shall, through reparation made by chosen souls, and through a new realization by all men of My kindness, of My mercy and of My love.

"My words will be light and life for an incalculable number of souls. They will all be printed, read and preached, and I will grant very special grace, that by them souls may be enlightened and transformed." (November 13, 1923).

"I wish to speak today to My consecrated religious, that they may make Me known to sinners and to the whole world.

"There are many among them who as yet are unable to understand My true feelings. They treat Me as One far away . . . known only slightly, and in whom they have too little confidence. I want them to rekindle their faith and love, and live trustfully in My intimacy, loving and loved.

"It is usually the eldest son of the family who best knows the mind and secret affairs of his father. In him the father is wont to confide more than in the younger ones, who as yet are unable to interest themselves in serious matters, or penetrate below the surface of things. So when the father comes to die, it behooves the eldest brother to transmit his wishes and will to these the younger ones.

"In My Church too, I have elder brothers: they are those whom I Myself have chosen, consecrated by the priesthood or by the vows of religion. They live nearest Me; they share in My choicest graces, and to them I confide My secrets, My desires . . . and My sufferings also. I have committed to them the care of My little children, their brothers, and through their ministry they must, directly or indirectly, guide them and transmit My teaching to them.

"If these chosen souls know Me truly, they will make Me known to others; if they love Me, they will make others love Me. But how can they teach their brethren if they hardly know Me themselves? I ask you: Can there be much love in the heart for One who is barely known? Or what intimate converse can be exchanged with One who is avoided . . . or in whom one has little confidence? . . .

"This is precisely what I wish to recall to the minds of My chosen ones. Nothing new, doubtless, but they have need to reanimate their faith, their love and their trust.

"I look for greater intimacy and confidence in the way they treat Me. Let them seek Me within their own hearts, for they know that a soul in a state of grace is the tabernacle of the Holy Spirit. And there, let them consider Me as I truly am, their God, but a God of love. Let love triumph over fear, and above all let them never forget that I love them. Many are convinced that it was because of this love that they were chosen, but when they are cast down at the sight of their miseries, of their faults even, then they grow sad at the thought that I have changed and love them less than before."   (December 4, 1923).

"How little such souls really know Me. They have not understood My Heart. For it is their very destitution and failings that incline My goodness towards them. And when acknowledging their helplessness and weakness, they humble themselves and have recourse to Me trustfully, then indeed they give Me more glory than before their fault.

"It is the same when they pray, either for themselves or for others; if they waver and doubt, they do not glorify My Heart, but they do glorify It, if they are sure that I shall give them what they ask, knowing that I refuse them nothing that is good for their souls.

"When the Centurion came to beg Me to cure his servant, he said very humbly: 'I am not worthy that Thou shouldst enter under my roof' . . . and faith and trust prevailing, he added: 'Say but the word, and my servant shall be healed.' This man knew My Heart. He knew that I could not resist the prayer of one who trusted Me absolutely. He gave Me much glory, for to humility he joined confidence. Yes, this man knew My Heart, yet I had made no manifestations to him as I have to My chosen ones.

"Hope obtains innumerable graces for self and for others. I want this to be thoroughly understood, so that My Heart's goodness may be revealed to those poor souls who as yet do not know Me.

"I once more repeat what I have already said, and it is nothing new: As a flame needs to be fed, if it is not to be extinguished, so souls need constant fresh urging to make them advance, and new warmth to reanimate them.

"Few among the souls that are consecrated to Me possess this unshakable confidence, because there are few that live in intimate union with Me. I want them to know that I love them as they are. I know that through frailty they will fall more than once, I know that they will often break the promises they have made Me. But their will to do better glorifies Me, their humble avowals after their falls, their trust in the forgiveness I will grant, glorify My Heart so much, that I will shower abundant graces on them.

"I want them all to know too how greatly I desire a renewal of their union and intimacy with Me. Let them not be satisfied with merely conversing with Me in church, where doubtless I am truly present, but remember that I abide in them, and delight in this union.

"Let them speak to Me of all their concerns . . . consult Me at every turn . . . ask favors of Me . . . I live in them to be their life . . . I abide in them to be their strength. Yes, I repeat, let them remember that I delight in being one with them . . . remember that I am in them . . . and that there I see them, hear them, love them.

There I look for a return from them.

"Many are accustomed to a daily meditation; but for how many it becomes a mere formality, instead of a loving interview . . . They say or assist at Mass and receive Me in Holy Communion, but on leaving the church become absorbed in their own interests to such an extent that they scarcely say a word to Me.

"I am in that soul as in a desert, she neither speaks to Me nor asks anything of Me . . . and when in need of comfort, she solicits it from creatures whom she must search out rather than from Me her Creator who abides and lives within her . . . Is not this want of union, want of interior spirit, in other words, want of love?

"Further, let Me once more tell those who are consecrated to Me how I specially chose them, that they might live in union with Me, to comfort Me and repair for the sins of those who offend Me.

"I want them to remember that it is their duty to study My Heart, in order to share in Its feelings, and as far as in their power, to realize Its desires.

"When a man works at his own field, how hard he toils at weeding it of all noxious growths, sparing neither trouble nor fatigue till he has attained his object. In like manner, as soon as My chosen ones know My desires, they should labor with zeal and ardor, undeterred by difficulty or suffering, that My glory may be increased and the sins of the world repaired."

(December 5, 1923).

"And now write for My consecrated souls:

"I call them all—My priests, My religious, and My nuns—to live a life of intimate union with Me.

"It is their privilege to know My longings and to share in My joys and sorrows.

"Theirs, to labor at My interests, never sparing themselves trouble or pain.

"Theirs, above all, to become more and more closely united to Me and never abandon Me; not to leave Me alone! Some do not understand and forget that it is for them to give Me companionship and consolation . . .

"And finally, it is for them to combine together in a league of love making but one in My Heart, to implore for souls the knowledge of truth, light and pardon. And when they see with deep sorrow the outrages I receive, My chosen souls will offer themselves to make reparation and to labor at My work; let their trust be unhesitating, for I shall not refuse their supplications, and all they ask shall be granted them.

"Let them all, then, apply themselves to the study of My Heart and to understand My feelings, striving to live in union with Me, to converse with Me and consult Me. Let them clothe their actions in My merits, bathe them in My Blood, and consecrate their lives to the saving of souls and the extension of My glory.

"Let them not descend to personal reflections which belittle them, but rejoice at seeing themselves clothed with the power of My Blood and of My merits. If they rely on self, they will do little or nothing, but if they labor with Me, in My Name and for My glory, they will be powerful.

"Let these consecrated souls revive their desire for reparation, and beg confidently for the advent of the divine King: that is, for My universal Sovereignty.

"Let them have no fear, let them hope in Me, let them trust in Me. Let them be burnt up with zeal and charity for sinners . . . praying for them with compassionate hearts and treating them with all gentleness.

"Let the world hear from their lips how great is My kindness, My love and My mercy.

"Armed with prayer, penance and reliance on Me, never on self, let them go forward to their apostolic labors in the power and goodness of My Heart which is ever with them . . .

"My Apostles were poor and ignorant men, but rich and wise in the wealth and wisdom of God, and their watchword was: In Thy Name, O Lord, I shall labor and be all-powerful.

"I ask three things of My consecrated souls:

Reparation, that is a life of union with Him who makes Divine Reparation: to work for Him, with Him, in Him, in a spirit of reparation, in close union with His feelings and desires.

Love, that is intimacy with Him who is all Love, and who humbles Himself to ask His creatures not to leave Him alone, but to give Him their love.

Confidence, that is trust in Him who is Goodness and Mercy . . . in Him with whom I live day and night . . . who knows me and whom I know . . . who loves me and whom I love . . . in Him who calls His chosen souls in a special way to live with Him, to know His Heart and so to trust Him for everything." (December 6, 1923).

THE WAY OF DIVINE LOVE. Sr. Josefa Menéndez. 504 pp. Paperbound. Imprimatur. One of the greatest spiritual classics of all time. A large part of this book comes from Our Lord Himself, as He reveals the secrets of His love for man to this humble 20th-century nun. This book makes lasting devotees of its readers, for Our Lord Himself promised in this book, "I tell you once more that grace will accompany My words and those who make them known. Truth will triumph and peace will reign over souls and the world." Her description of Hell, written under obedience, is alone worth the price of the book.
0104 Quality paperbound edition.　　　　　**21.50**

I WAIT FOR YOU—Jesus' Lament over Man's Indifference. 32 pp. PB. Imprimatur. Jesus' own powerful words from *The Way of Divine Love* showing His great love for souls and His displeasure over mankind's neglect of His love, especially of His Eucharistic Presence. (5–1.00 ea.; 10–.80 ea.; 25–.70 ea.; 50–.60 ea.; 100–.50 ea.; 500–.40 ea.; 1,000–.30 ea.).
No. 1026.　　　　　**1.50**